ESL
Picture
Dictionary

US Edition

Peak Educational 2022

ESL Picture Dictionary
United States Edition
© Peak Educational 2022

Photo Attributions:

All images in this publication are licensed under a CC0 (Public Domain) license, except the following:

Speech Bubbles by icon 54 from the Noun Project, Question by Delwar Hossain from the Noun Project
Page 11: Two-hole German Hole Punch byTom Yeshuah
https://commons.wikimedia.org/wiki/File:Two-hole_German_Hole_Punch.JPG CC BY-SA 3.0
Page 12: FLATSEVEN Mens Slim Fit Designer Casual Trench Coat by FLATSEVEN
https://www.flickr.com/photos/flatseven/34772535193 CC-BY-SA 2.0 Page 29: Toothache
https://www.flickr.com/photos/156555495@N04/41891124385 by Free For Commercial Use (FFC)
CC BY 2.0 Page 29: Coughing https://www.flickr.com/photos/57638320@N00/15058305422 CC BY
2.0 by GabboT
Page 34: SAUCEPAN by Marco Verch
https://foto.wuestenigel.com/saucepan/?utm_source=38499485241&utm_campaign=FlickrDescripti
on&utm_medium=link CC-BY-SA 2.0 Page 35: Ikea Billy Bookcase CC-BY-SA 2.0 By Faruk Ates
https://www.flickr.com/photos/kurafire/6948563610
Page 40: Shop assistant, 2 oceans acquaria, by flowcomm
https://www.flickr.com/photos/flowcomm/4486348806 CC-BY-SA 2.0
Page 44: British museum by Ham
https://commons.wikimedia.org/wiki/File:British_Museum_from_NE_2.JPG CC BY-SA 3.0
Page 44: Greyhound buses at depot:
https://en.wikipedia.org/wiki/File:Greyhound_buses_at_depot_-
_Portland,_Oregon.JPG#/media/File:Greyhound_buses_at_depot_-_Portland,_Oregon.JPG

Every effort has been made to correctly attribute the images. Please send any enquiries to:
peakeducationaluk@gmail.com

Contents

ESL Picture Dictionary

Welcome

"How do you spell this?" is probably one of the most common questions ESL* students ask teachers during their courses.

Many students are at the beginning of their journey towards being able to read and write.

Classes which involve spelling or writing activities are especially difficult and anxiety-inducing for these learners.

The **ESL Picture Dictionary** is designed to help beginner literacy ESL students access spelling for the words they are likely to encounter in their classes.

It also provides a direct, visual way to acquire new vocabulary without the need of translation in multilingual classroom environments.

Words are arranged in alphabetical order within each topic. The topics selected are not exhaustive but ones which students are very likely to come across in their beginning ESOL courses.

* English as a Second Language

Action
Verbs

ask	cut	cry
dance	drink	drive
eat	give	laugh

Action Verbs

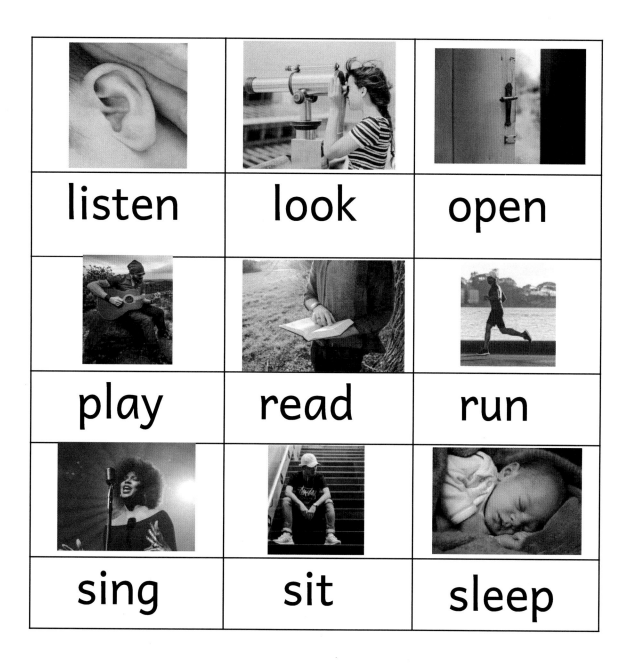

listen	look	open
play	read	run
sing	sit	sleep

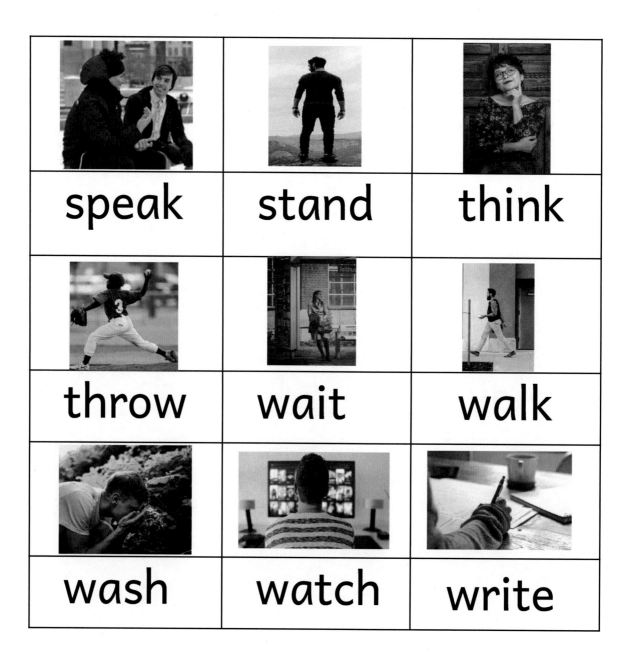

speak	stand	think
throw	wait	walk
wash	watch	write

Classroom

binder	book	eraser
hole punch	notebook	pen
pencil	scissors	stapler

Classroom

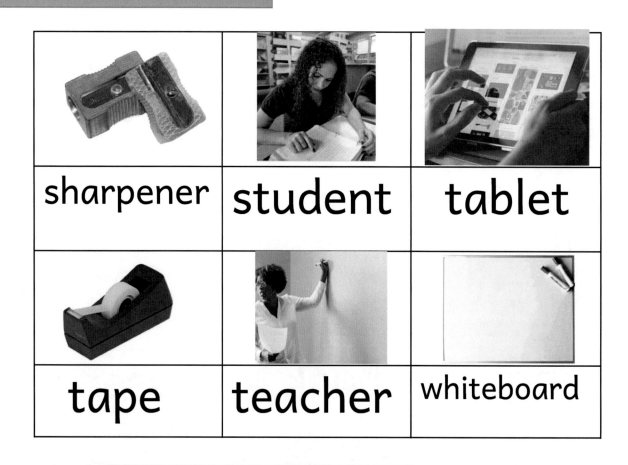

sharpener	student	tablet
tape	teacher	whiteboard

talk box 💬

 *Do you have a hole punch please?*

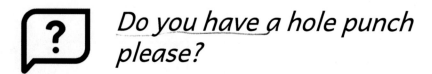 Pass me the blue pen please.

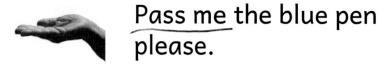 *What is it?*

It is a stapler.

Clothes

belt	cap	coat
dress	glasses	gloves
hat	jacket	jeans

jewelry	necklace	pajamas
rings	scarf	shirt
shoes	skirt	socks
suit	T- shirt	tie

Clothes

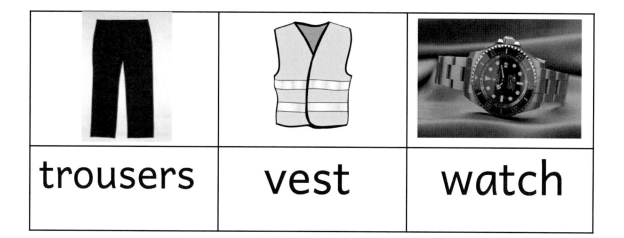		
trousers	vest	watch

talk box

 What are you wearing?

 I'm wearing a red jumper and scarf.

 In the morning, I **get dressed.**

 I **put on** my shoes.

 I **hang** my clothes in the **closet.**

Colors

⚫	⚫	⚫
black	blue	brown
⚫	⚫	⚫
gold	green	gray
⚫	⚫	⚫
orange	pink	purple

Colours

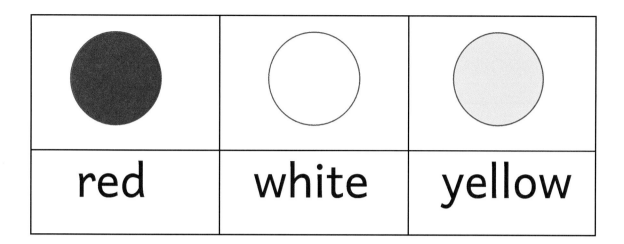		
red	white	yellow

talk box

? *What color is it?*
It is yellow.

? *What color are they?*
They are red.

? *What is your favorite colour?*
My favourite color is blue.

Days of the week

7 days

1.	Monday
2.	Tuesday
3.	Wednesday
4.	Thursday
5.	Friday
6.	Saturday
7.	Sunday

Every day

brush my teeth	clean the house	cook
get dressed	go shopping	go to work
have breakfast	have dinner	take a shower

wake up	wash the dishes	watch TV

talk box

 What time do you wake up?

 I wake up at 7.00am.

  How often do you cook?

 I cook once a day.

Family

aunt	baby	brothers
cousins	daughter	father
grandfather	grandmother	husband

Family

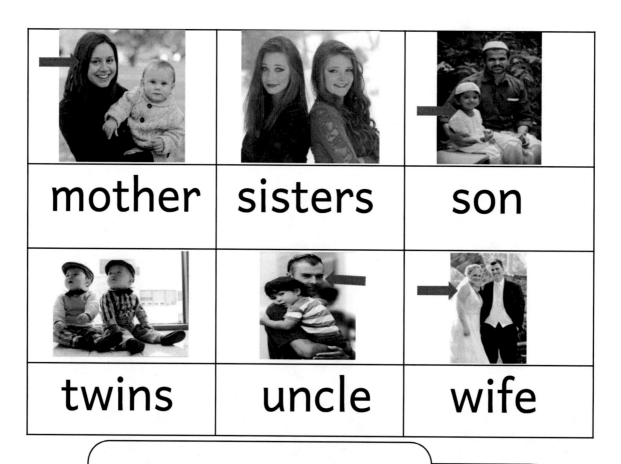

mother	sisters	son
twins	uncle	wife

? *How many children do you have?*

 We have 2 children.

 I have 1 son and 1 daughter.

Feelings

Feelings

angry	bored	calm
excited	happy	lonely
in love	proud	sad

scared	shocked	tired

talk box

 *How do you feel?*

I feel tired.

? *How does he feel?*

➕ He feels happy.

➖ He doesn't feel sad.

Food:
fruit

apple	banana	dates
fig	grapes	lemon
lime	mango	orange

Food

papaya	peach	pear
pineapple	plums	pomegranate
strawberry	raspberry	watermelon

Food:
vegetables

artichoke	asparagus	bell pepper
broccoli	cabbage	carrot
cauliflower	cucumber	eggplant

Food

garlic	lettuce	mushrooms
onion	potato	sweetcorn
sweet potato	tomato	zucchini

Food:
meat

beef	chicken	duck
fish	ground meat	lamb
pork	sausage	turkey

Health:
problems

backache	broken arm	broken leg
a cold	a cough	headache
stomach ache	sore throat	toothache

Health:
people

doctor	dentist	midwife
nurse	patient	paramedic
pharmacist	receptionist	surgeon

Home:
types of houses

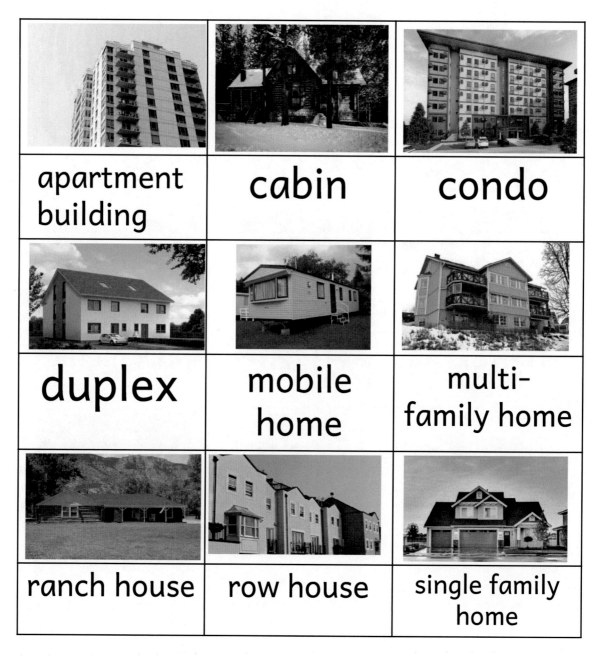

apartment building	cabin	condo
duplex	mobile home	multi-family home
ranch house	row house	single family home

Home:
rooms in the house

attic	bathroom	bedroom
dining room	garden	hall
kitchen	living room	study

Home:
in the kitchen

bowl	blender	coffee maker
cup	cupboard	dishwasher
kettle	knife	microwave

mop	oven	pan
plate	refrigerator	sink
spoon	toaster	whisk

Home:
in the living room

armchair	bookcase	coffee table
curtains	cushions	pictures
rug	sofa	television

Home:
in the bathroom

bathtub	faucet	mirror
shower	soap	sink basin
toothbrush	towel	toilet

Home:
in the bedroom

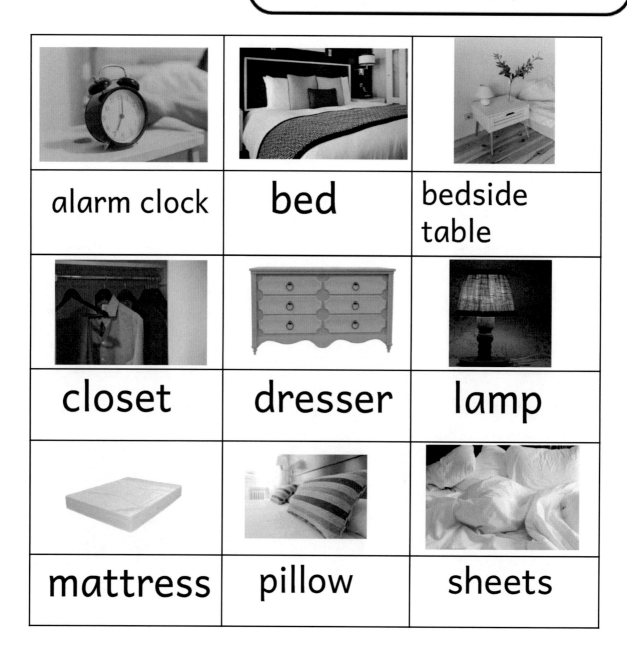

alarm clock	bed	bedside table
closet	dresser	lamp
mattress	pillow	sheets

talk box

? *What type of house do you live in?*

I live in a row house.

? *How many bedrooms are there?*

There are 4 bedrooms.

? *Which floor do you live on?*

I live on the 4th floor.

Jobs

barber	beautician	builder
chef	delivery driver	engineer
firefighter	mechanic	pilot

police officer	plumber	security guard
shop assistant	taxi driver	teacher

talk box 💬

? *What's your job?*

I'm a builder

Months of the year

12 months

1.	January
2.	February
3.	March
4.	April
5.	May
6.	June
7.	July
8.	August
9.	September
10.	October
11.	November
12.	December

Numbers:
cardinal

1	one
2	two
3	three
4	four
5	five
6	six
7	seven
8	eight
9	nine
10	ten

11	eleven
12	twelve
13	thirteen
14	fourteen
15	fifteen
16	sixteen
17	seventeen
18	eighteen
19	nineteen
20	twenty

30	thirty
40	forty
50	fifty
60	sixty
70	seventy
80	eighty
90	ninety

100	one hundred
150	one hundred and fifty
1000	one thousand
1,250	one thousand, two hundred and fifty

Numbers:
ordinal

1st	first	11th	eleventh
2nd	second	12th	twelfth
3rd	third	13th	thirteenth
4th	fourth	14th	fourteenth
5th	fifth	15th	fifteenth
6th	sixth	20th	twentieth
7th	seventh	21st	twenty-first
8th	eighth	22nd	twenty-second
9th	ninth	23rd	twenty-third
10th	tenth	30th	thirtieth

Places
in the city

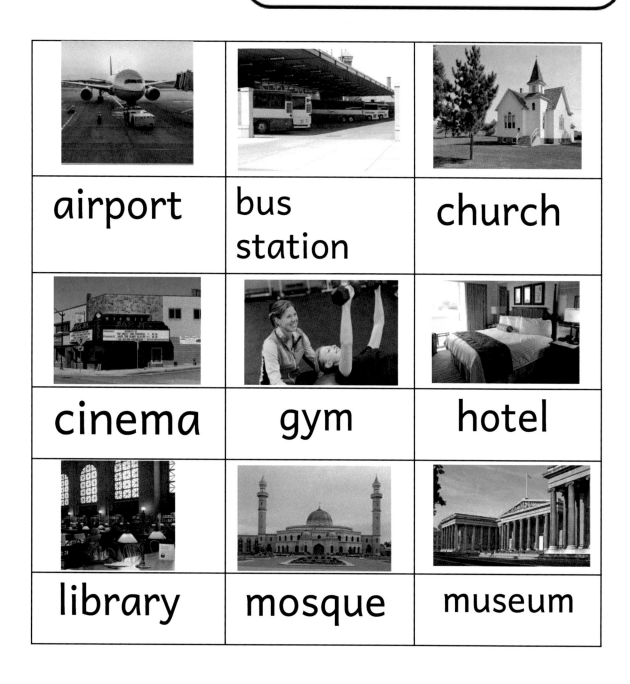

airport	bus station	church
cinema	gym	hotel
library	mosque	museum

Places

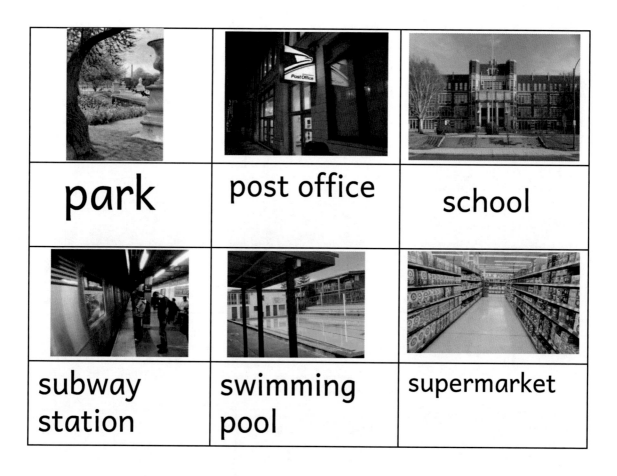

park	post office	school
subway station	swimming pool	supermarket

talk box 💬

  Where is the library?

The library is in the city center, next to the park.

Shopping

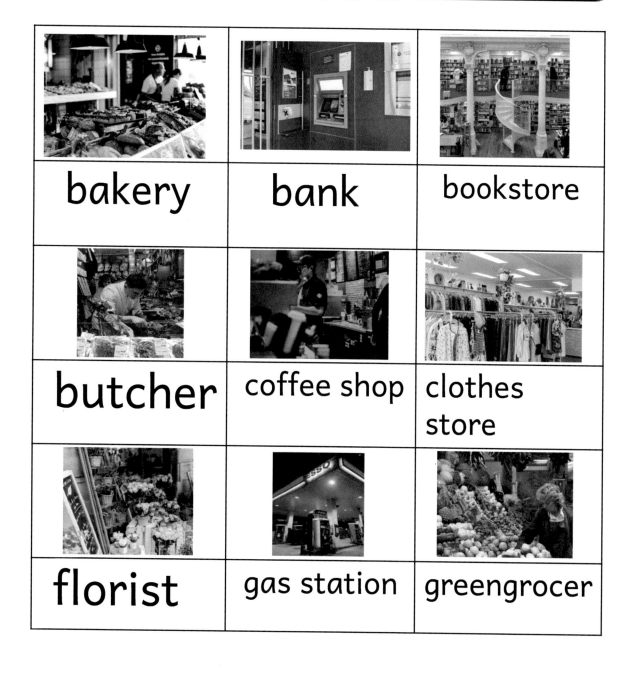

bakery	bank	bookstore
butcher	coffee shop	clothes store
florist	gas station	greengrocer

Shopping

 hairdresser	jeweler	laundromat
market	pharmacy	toy shop

talk box 💬

? *Where can I buy paracetamol?*

At the pharmacy.

? *Where can I buy a birthday cake?*

At the bakery.

Transportation

airplane	ambulance	bicycle
boat	bus	car
fire truck	helicopter	motorcycle

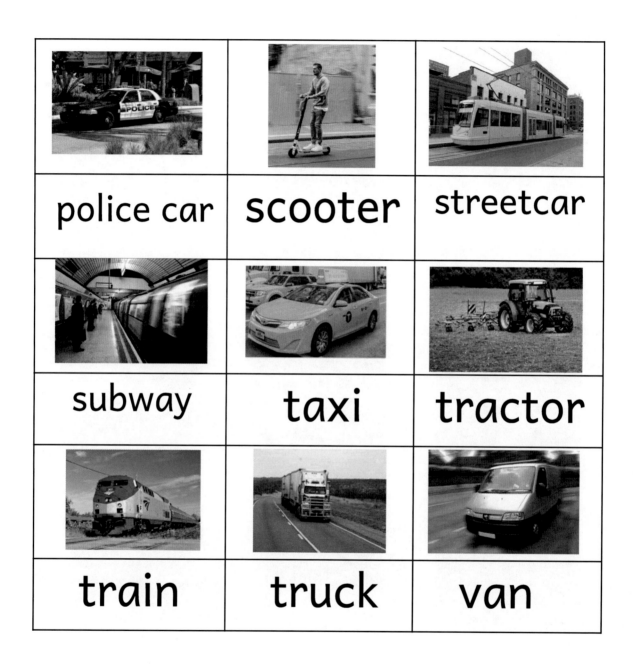

police car	scooter	streetcar
subway	taxi	tractor
train	truck	van

Weather

cloudy	cold	foggy
hot	icy	rainy
snow	storm	sunny

warm	wet	windy

talk box

? *What's the weather like today?*

It's cloudy.

? *What's the temperature?*

It's 60 degrees (60° F)

? *What type of weather do you prefer?*

I **prefer** sunny weather.

Made in the USA
Las Vegas, NV
05 April 2023

70200368R00031